When You Need A Miracle

PRAY

WHEN YOU NEED A MIRACLE - PRAY

Copyright © 2015 D. Ashanti-Dubois

Premier Edition Published in 2015 in the United States of America

ALL RIGHTS RESERVED.

No part of this publication; including photos, may be reproduced, stored, or transmitted by any means; including electronic, digital, or manual, nor by photocopy, fax, video, or recording without the written permission of the publisher and author. Exception given for brief quotations in printed reviews.

Cover design Copyright © 2015 D. Ashanti-Dubois

All photos Copyright © 2015 D. Ashanti-Dubois, My Dove Song Publishing

My Dove Song Publishing is the exclusive licensee of all photographs used in this publication.

WWW.MYDOVESONG.COM

ISBN-13: 978-0692022030
ISBN-10: 0692022031

WHEN YOU NEED A MIRACLE PRAY

D. ASHANTI-DUBOIS

MyDoveSong
MYDOVESONG
PUBLISHING

Thank you, Lord, for watching over me. You have been my refuge in every moment of my life. When the darkness overtake me and I can't seem to escape its doom, your grace falls on me. You are my shelter by day and you shield me and in my hour of need. I lay down every problem of my life before you. Every worry in my heart and every fear that plagues my soul, I place in your hands. I rest in you, for you are peace. Amen.

Maui, Hawaii - Kula

help me, Father God... I need your guidance. Grant me wisdom in my decisions and give me your vision so that I know what I must do. And when I am lost in confusion, help me to see my way clear. When I am lost in darkness, I pray that your hand will guide me. You, oh, Lord, you have a solution to every problem and you provide for my every need. Help me to be more loving and wise, and keep me in your tender care. Amen.

Holy Father, please deliver me from trouble. Descend upon my life and bless me with your gift of faith. I need you, Lord. I lift my voice to praise you, for only you provide for me. Only you can deliver me. Grant me courage, faith and hope, for through your might I draw my strength. You are Holy and your presence is Divine. You are my God and I wait on you. Lift my head and deliver me to your heavenly peace. Amen.

Maui, Hawaii - Hana

Healing to Survive

Father, you alone keep me from falling when the whole world is falling apart. Lord, when I am sad, you comfort me. When I am weak, you raise me up. You are my way tout of no way. On your strength alone I stand. You are the wall between me and poverty, illness, and disease; only your grace can heal. Have mercy on me, Lord, for I cannot make it alone. I need you desperately. Heal me in the name of Jesus Christ. Amen.

Guéthary, France - Pays Basque

Lord, please forgive me for everything I've done wrong. Empty me of all that is unclean and make my life acceptable to you. Fill me with your mercy and Holy love. Take me and make me what I should be. Cleanse me and heal me of all that is not pleasing to you. Pardon the words I've spoken in anger, and the hurt I've caused to others. I am asking for your forgiveness. Pardon me. Let me stand in your presence today. Amen.

Maui, Hawaii - Kahalui

Lord God, I need a miracle in my life. Please lift me out of sorrow and show me the way to rise above my circumstances. Your wisdom is mighty and your compassion is great. If there is a door that I can't open, open it for me. If there is a window that leads to my destruction, please bar it from me. Guide me to your everlasting peace, and allow me to live in dignity. Provide for all of my needs. I praise you forever. Amen.

My heavenly Father, have mercy on me. I am lost in the wilderness, but when I call on you, you comfort me. In the blink of an eye I feel your presence near. When I feel so alone and my heart suffers in pain, I know, oh God, that you have never left me, for you have kept me time in and time out; sun up and sun down. Thank you for loving me. Thank you for bringing me peace and for sending your Holy Spirit to comfort me. Amen.

Anglet, France - Forêt de Chiberta

Healing Anger

Bless me, oh Lord, for I need you now. Protect me with your healing hand and lead me to a place of peace. Troubles bring me down and anger rises up, but oh, Holy Divine, you wipe away my fears. The worry and pain, anger and distress all disappear when I place my mind on you. Hurtful things have no place in me because they do not come from you. Grant me peace and healing this very hour. I praise you, Lord, forever...

Anglet, France - Forêt de Chiberta

You are the keeper of my soul. You are my God; my sweet deliverer. Only good is found in you. And though I stumble and fall, your grace saves me. Even though I am bitter-sweet and salty to the taste, you look at me through eyes of love. You comfort me like honey and care for me, yet I am imperfect in every way. Bless me with your Holy presence and send your angels to watch over me. Lord, bless me this day... Amen.

Anglet, France - Forêt de Chiberta

Mercy

Lift me, oh Lord, for I am down on my knees. I lay my head upon your feet and cry out your Holy name. This life is not easy, fill me your precious peace. Heal me, Savior, for only you can deliver me. Thank you for your mercy though I've done things for which I am ashamed. But you, Father, forgive my faults and my past, and love me unconditionally. Through your perfect love, I am healed. Have mercy; I'm calling on you...

Guéthary, France - Pays Basque

Heal me Master, my sacred Lord. My body is weak, but you are strong. Grant my life your abiding peace. Send your love and comfort me. I thank you, Lord, for this day and for everything you have done for me. You are worthy of all praise. Where would I be if it weren't for your grace? You have kept me from falling and I thank you for your love. You are a generous and loving God. Bless my soul and heal me now. Amen.

Guéthary, France - Pays Basque

Hope

You are my Heavenly Father, my blessed sacred hope. Touch my life with love and fill me up with mercy. Lord, I am so thankful for my life. You have taken away my pain and replaced it with faith. You have kept my mind and soul and have given me Divine peace. You are my Lord and Savior, my hope in times of trouble. You are my strength and my deliverer. I praise your name for all you have done for me. You are my God...

Guéthary, France - Pays Basque

Precious Lord, where would I be if you were not in my life? Through every storm, though I was afraid, you comforted me and kept me safe. You forgave my faults and teach me your ways. Through your grace, I have survived, for you have provided for me. You give me sustenance and give me peace. You guide me when I'm awake and protect me when I am asleep. You deliver me from my troubles, and I thank you for my life. Amen.

Anglet, France - Chambre d'Amour

Heavenly Father, my heart is aching and I don't know where to turn. Sorrow has overtaken me; I am worn and feel so alone. Lord, I look to you... I need your presence close to me. Help me climb my mountain. I need your strength to make it through. Please deliver my feigning spirit and turn my darkest days into joyful morns. Come, Holy Spirit, and grant me peace through the eye of the storm. Strengthen me, oh Lord. Amen.

Anglet, France - Chambre d'Amour

Oh, Holy One, please hear my cry. I am on my knees and need you now. My enemies are set against me, and those whom I trusted are corrupt. I cannot make it all alone. Lord, you are my only hope. Father, you know what I am going through. I lay my troubles before your feet. Master, I know you can deliver me. Change my situations; even change me. I need your help, my Heavenly Father. I need you Lord, today. Amen.

Pays Basque, France - La Rhune

Take my hand, Lord, and lead me as I walk this road. I place all my trust in you. Thank you for letting me see another day and for the grace that you have given me. Thank you for keeping for me; and keep my loved ones safe. Lord, you are my Everlasting Father and my deliverer. Master without you I would never make it through this life. Thank you for giving me your eternal peace. I praise your glorious name forever. Amen.

La Rhune, France - Pays Basque

Lord, thank you so much for all you have done for me. You have kept me through the good times and protected me through the bad. And because of your grace, I have enough to eat and a place to lay my head. And though sometimes the days are long and my nights are filled with tears, I wake with my heart filled with hope for I have triumphed over the dark. You were with me and kept me, and I thank you, Lord. Amen.

Maui, Hawaii

Oh, how I need you, Christ Jesus, when the world is set against me and tears are falling down my cheeks. You are the one I cling to when I feel trapped in misery. Lord, you to lift my soul so that I may feel joy in my heart. You take away my worries and ease my mind with faith. You guide all my footsteps that I may live my life in truth. Help me to be more loving, and give me your Holy strength. Lift me up in victory this day. Amen.

Oh, Lord, my God, heal me with your Divine love and make me whole again. I am bowed down low, breathe life into my soul and make me reborn. Take these shackles and free my spirit; heal me from the pain. Raise me up, free my mind, and deliver me from all shame. I come to you for I have no where else to go. I stand on the promises of faith and your everlasting hope. Please bring peace to my life. In Jesus name I pray. Amen.

Anglet, France - Chambre d'Amour

Lord, please look inside my heart and change my ways. Help me to be more like you. I wish I could undo many of the things I have already done, but if you just wash away all the hurt and pain and take away all that is not of you, my life will be renewed. Free me of these burdens; I am tired of my imperfect ways. Lord, just lift me up and make me whole again. I want to live my life in peace. I want to be whole in you. Amen.

Anglet, France - Chambre d'Amour

Lord, help me to be the person that I need to be. Calm me and give me inner-peace. Grant me patience and help me to handle the stresses of my daily life. Lord, I want to be able to listen and not get angry, to speak and not be rude; to live and not regret. I want to be more loving; to treat others as you treat me. Please take away all within me that is not pleasing to you. I want to be more like you. In Jesus name I pray... Amen.

Maui, Hawaii

Lord, all blessings comes from you. Sometimes, I feel so alone and you comfort me. I say the wrong things and make many mistakes, yet you love me. You pick me up when I am down. You gather me when I am falling apart. You hold me when I am in the cold. You bless me when life is cruel. Lord, I want to be forever in your presence. I never want to be without you. For all the blessings you have bestowed on my life, I thank you...

Cinq Cantons - Anglet, France

Guidance

Lord, let my mouth speak your wishes and my heart reflect your love. Let me be wise in my decisions, and forgiving in my heart. Let me choose the roads you have destined for me and avoid the ones where I will fall. Lord, in you I put my trust and release what separates me from your will. I glorify you and magnify your name with my small insignificant voice. You are my God and I believe in you. May your will be done. Amen.

Maui, Hawaii - Hana

Heavenly Father, grant me clarity in my situation. Give me the right things to say, and allow my spirit to be one of peace, wisdom, and competence. Let others see the love in me and treat me fairly and kind. Bring out the best in me, Lord. Let me possess your spirit of hope. Let me be the parent, friend, co-worker and family that is understanding, patient, loving, faithful, and kind. Help others to see your love in me. Amen.

Maui, Hawaii

When I am weak, you make me strong. Lord, when I have fallen, you lift me up and show me the way. I've been alone shivering in the dark, and you brought me into the light. You healed me, Lord. You were my only salvation. Without you, where would I be? You found me barren in the wilderness without a dime to my name, and you rescued me. And I shall forever lift my voice to praise you, for you have given me new life.

Maui, Hawaii

Lord, I'm going to keep praising you. I'm going to keep worshipping you. I'm going to keep magnifying your name for all you've done for me. I want to thank you for saving my life. I want to thank you for the blessings I couldn't do without. You saved me from myself and every one else. You've been so good I want to holler and shout. I thank you for all you've done for me. I'm going to praise you because you set me free...

Maui, Hawaii

Thank you, Father, for this day. Help me to reach all my goals and not turn towards the wrong, but towards the righteous path. Help me to be free of my fear and walk in your light. Lord, I am your child, and I pray that you walk with me and shield me. I ask that my heart be delivered from trouble and my life made whole. I ask you to guide me and protect me, even from myself. Keep me safe and deliver me from harm. Amen.

Maui, Hawaii - Wailuku

please deliver me from circumstances; make me whole again. Take care of me. Stand with me and hold my hand. You are my hope; my only source of joy. You are my strength, Lord. Hold me in your arms. Father God, I need you. I need near me now. Let me lay in your arms of grace. Please take my tears away. Amen.

Maui, Hawaii - Hana

Lord, thank you for letting me live to see one more day. Father God, my life is in your hands. Watch over and guide me that I may do your will. In everything I do and all that I live, let me be peaceful, loving, and happy. Guard from disease, frustration, ridicule, and anger. Bind my tongue that I may not say what I will regret. Lord, lift me when I am feeling low and bind my wounds that I may feel your blessings on my life. Amen.

Father, let your love rain over me. Lord, I need your will in my life. Please calm my fears with your everlasting peace and fill my heart with compassion and understanding. Lord, help me to be all that I dream, and help me to attain my goals. On this day and every day of my life please walk with me, so that I may overcome this world. Lift me up. Keep me close... Lord, I need a miracle in my life, and that miracle is you... Amen.

Maui, Hawaii - Kihei

Replace my loneliness with love, my frailty with strength, my fears with faith, my doubts with courage, and my tears with joy. Wrap me in your arms of love and surround me with your grace. Heavenly Father, touch my heart and my life, so that I may live in peace. Let hope be my battle cry and strength be my armor. Gird me with courage and let me be unafraid of what lies ahead. Grant me this blessing in Jesus name... Amen.

Thank you for this beautiful day, Lord. Thank you for all the blessing on my life. You woke me up this morning and protected me through the night. You guided my footsteps and kept me when I went astray. Because of your grace, I can pray in my right mind. How blessed I am to have your love. This world my test my faith, but your love is everywhere. Thank you for protecting me. Only your grace have kept me safe...

Guéthary, France - Pays Basque

Happiness

Lord, let me feel your joy and your strength. Let your sun shine upon me. Let the wind blow through my hair. Let me live like love is water and have believe like my faith is bread. Let me nourish my soul in laughter and let work until dreams come true. Let me build a life of happiness without fear or worry. Let me wake with only hope for tomorrow and sleep with my heart open wide. Let me live in happiness; let me live in you...

Guéthary, France - Pays Basque

Miracles

I give my all to you, Lord; to walk in faith and leave behind my tears. Lord, let me be inside your mercy and live inside your love. Deliver my soul from sorrow. Grant me a miracle by faith. Lift my head that I may see the promises life holds for me. Open my heart to the present and close the door to the painful past. I need a miracle in my life. I put all my trust in you. Please grant me my heart's desire. I will always praise you. Amen.

Anglet, France - Chambre d'Amour

My Lord, open a door to my happiness. Many have been closed in my face. Lord, you hold the key to my deliverance. Only you, Father, can get me through this difficult time. I feel like an empty wind blowing through a valley, but where ever you want me, that is where I wish to be. Please surround me with your love and bind me in your heart. I want to be forever in your will. Deliver me this day... Amen.

Maui, Hawaii - Kula

Lord, keep me in your tender care... Watch over my loved ones so that we may feel your holy presence. Lord, keep us safe and free from harm. Walk with us in our daily lives, and guide us towards our dreams. Lift us up so that we may feel your glory and be secure in your arms. Father, please be with us in every way; in our hearts and in our minds that we may receive your blessings in our lives. In Jesus name I pray... Amen.

La Rhune, France - Pays Basque

Righteousness

Heavenly Father, teach me right from wrong. Lead me to the path of righteousness and make me a follower of your ways. Teach me to be strong and help me to understand your will for my life. Speak to my heart that I may know your voice, and guide me with your hand. Without you, Lord, I do not know which way is up or what is down. This world is filled with confusion, but in you, I see my way clear. Thank you for my faith...

Protection

Lord, watch over my children... Make them vessels of your love. Keep them safe from their enemies. Give them wisdom, courage, and love. Let them be guided by their faith and protected from their fears. Let them be saved by your amazing grace. Let their anger dissolve into empathy and their character be beyond reproach. Let them know where to turn when they need help and let them turn to you. In Jesus name...Amen.

Almighty redeemer, cover me with your grace. When pain overtakes me and life overwhelms me, I know you won't forsake me. And I know that you are there, because every time I call you, I feel you draw near. You send the angels to comfort me and they watch over me as I pray. You are so good to me, Lord. You help me through the bad times and I endure. With you, I rise again, even after I fall. Thank you, for loving me...

Heavenly Father, I raise my hands in praise to you. There is no one like you in all the earth, for only you can heal my pain so I sing praises to your name for your love and power are great. My voice cries out, though I am worn from the fight. You, Lord, are my hope. Where else can I turn, but to your everlasting love? Who else can hear my suffering? For you are my God and only you can deliver. I pray for eternal peace... Amen

ALWAYS BELIEVE.

If I can inspire a heart to beat again, or breathe life into a dream;

hearten those who cry in the night and bring them the morning sun,

then my journey was worth the tears, and I triumphed in the midst of them all.

-D. Ashanti-Dubois

ABOUT THE AUTHOR

Author and creative artist, D. Ashanti-Dubois, brings light and love to the universe of literature through her latest edition, When You Need A Miracle– Pray. As a multifaceted writer, photographer, vocalist, composer, graphic artist, and inspirational speaker, D. Ashanti-Dubois brings a unique perspective to the world of spiritual enlightenment. After nearly two decades of living internationally and in Hawaii, her intrepid journey has emboldened her belief in the spirit of hope, love, and humanity.

Born and raised in St. Louis, Missouri where she began her creative journey writing poetry, prose, and songs at the tender age of five, D. Ashanti-Dubois continues her artistic odyssey producing various genres of books, music, photography, and art.

Her spiritual anthology, *Messages of Hope,* is a collection of beautifully written spiritual insights to inspire and empower your life. The entire Messages of Hope series can be purchased online through Amazon.com and other vendors. Also available: *Messages of Hope – Words to Uplift the Human Spirit:* An uplifting book of 33 inspirational messages and 36 exercises to change in your life along with more than 150 gorgeous original photographs. *Messages d'Amour–Reflections of Love:* A romantic diary of love poems with gorgeous floral photography to inspire love and romance. *Heaven & Earth:* A magnificent collection of spiritual poetry and nature photography.

For more books available by D. Ashanti-Dubois visit www.mydovesong.com. Look for other editions scheduled to be released in the coming years.